# THE WRITE STUFF

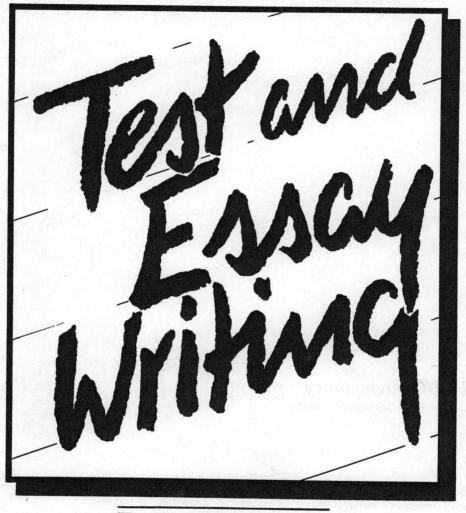

Test and Essay Writing

## Exercise Book

Project Editor—*Ellen Carley Frechette*

**McGraw-Hill/Contemporary**
A Division of The McGraw-Hill Companies

*McGraw-Hill/Contemporary*
A Division of *The McGraw·Hill Companies*

Send all inquiries to:
McGraw-Hill/Contemporary
4255 W. Touhy Ave.
Lincolnwood, IL 60712

ISBN: 0-8092-5100-0

Printed in the United States of America.

1 2 3 4 5 6 7 GB(M)   26 25 24 23 22 21 20 19 18 17

# CONTENTS

# NOTES TO THE INSTRUCTOR

Many students think of writing as a two-step process—you think of what you want to say and you write it down. However, this approach to writing can lead to ineffective prose. Some students will write lengthy essays "off the top of their heads"—essays that are often disorganized and unclear. Other students will be so concerned with grammar, spelling, and punctuation that they will be unable to get their thoughts onto paper. Both of these problems usually stem from a lack of understanding of the process of writing.

Your students need to know that most writing they see has been planned, changed, and rewritten several times before they even see it. They need to look at writing as a step-by-step process, not a "one-shot, get it right the first time" deal. The exercises in *Test and Essay Writing* will give students practice in prewriting, writing, and revising—each of the steps that are necessary to come up with clear and effective prose.

The exercises in this book can serve as supplementary activities to those in *Putting It in Paragraphs* and *Writing for a Purpose*, the instructional texts from *The Write Stuff* series. They move the student through the various stages of the writing process and give practice in four types of expository prose writing: narrative, descriptive, persuasive, and informative. Of course, a more experienced writer may be able to use the exercise book alone. In addition to reinforcing general writing skills, the book contains specific hints and techniques that will be useful for students who will be taking an essay test.

Writing students should be encouraged to use everything they've learned about the writing process. By carefully working through the activities in this book and reviewing the instructional texts of *The Write Stuff* series, they should be well prepared for many different kinds of in-class essay assignments and essay test situations.

# WARM-UP AND PREWRITING

Many people think that writing is a two-step process—you think of what you want to say, then you write it down.

Experienced writers realize that good writing consists of several different steps. You don't have to decide exactly what you're going to say before you start writing. You have lots of opportunities to think up ideas, write them down, and change them.

The exercises in this section will help you see some different ways to get started writing. They will also show you how you can organize your writing so that your reader can easily understand you.

## EXERCISE 1

# FOCUSING ON YOUR TOPIC

Before you can start writing, you need to have an idea of what you want to write about. In other words, you need to decide on your *topic*. Many times, especially on essay assignments and tests, your topic has already been given to you. Other times, your purpose for writing tells you your topic. For example, when you need to write a note to a repairman, you don't really need to sit down and think up a topic. Your topic is a given—a leaky faucet, a door that won't close, or a broken window. In still other instances, you may have to choose your own topic to write about.

However you arrive at your topic, the next step is to decide *what you want to say about this topic.* For example, if your topic is poverty, what do you want to say about poverty? What do you plan to write about it? Once you have decided this, you have a start into the writing process.

Notice that a topic can be written about in many different ways, depending upon what you, the writer, want to say. Although each of the following sentences is about poverty, imagine how different an essay based on each topic sentence would be!

> Poverty is the single most devastating problem in the United States today.
>
> When I was young, poverty forced me to see some of the harsh realities of the world.
>
> The visions of poverty in that small village are almost indescribable.

The writers of these sentences each had something different to say about poverty, and therefore each of their essays would be very different.

In this exercise, ask yourself *what you want to say* about each of the given topics. Write a sentence that tells what you want to say. Make sure that you write a complete sentence. The first one is done for you.

**1.** child abuse

*Child abuse is a crime that should be dealt with severely.*

_____

**2.** freedom

_____

_____

**3.** Chinese restaurants

_____

_____

**4.** your mother

_____

_____

**5.** the view from the top of a tall building

_____

_____

**6.** divorce

_____

_____

**7.** partying

_____

_____

**8.** God

_____

_____

**9.** the police

_____

_____

# EXERCISE 2

# WRITING A TOPIC SENTENCE

Most writing is formed in **paragraphs.** A paragraph is a group of sentences that all relate to the same idea.

Every paragraph needs a topic sentence that states the main idea of the paragraph. The **topic sentence** lets the reader know what the rest of the paragraph will be about. It sums up the *main idea* of the paragraph. In this exercise, you will practice writing topic sentences for different situations.

Read each situation below and think about what you would write for each paragraph. Then, on the lines provided, write a good topic sentence that would tell the main idea of the paragraph you would write. The first one is done for you.

After you have written all of the topic sentences, choose <u>one</u> and write a paragraph based on it.

**1.** You are asked on a writing test to give your opinion on the issue of mandatory use of seat belts in automobiles.

   TOPIC SENTENCE: *Wearing a seat belt is a personal issue, and it should not be required by law.*

**2.** You have been receiving magazines that you did not order. You write to the publisher to ask that it stop delivery.

   TOPIC SENTENCE:_____

   _____

**3.** A friend writes to you asking if he can stay at your apartment the next time he comes through town. You want to tell him that you have no room for him.

   TOPIC SENTENCE:_____

   _____

**4.** You lose your dog during a vacation in another state. You want the Anti-Cruelty Society in that state to look for your dog.

   TOPIC SENTENCE:_____

   _____

5. Most of the streetlights on your block are broken, and you want to tell the mayor how you feel about the situation.

TOPIC SENTENCE:_____

_____

6. You receive a bill for $200 from the phone company for a two-hour call to New Zealand. You don't even <u>know</u> anyone in New Zealand. You want to explain to the phone company why you won't pay the bill.

TOPIC SENTENCE:_____

_____

7. You are designing a poster for your department showing where the fire exits are. An artist is helping you, and you want to tell her how the poster should look.

TOPIC SENTENCE:_____

_____

8. You are filling out a job application, and you are asked to explain why you left your previous job.

TOPIC SENTENCE:_____

_____

PARAGRAPH:_____

_____

_____

_____

_____

_____

_____

_____

_____

_____

# WRITING A TOPIC SENTENCE FOR A GIVEN PARAGRAPH

Each paragraph below is missing a topic sentence. First, read each paragraph. Ask yourself what the topic is and what is being said about the topic. Think about the way all of the ideas in the paragraph are related. Then, on the lines provided, write a topic sentence that sums up the main idea of the paragraph. The first one is done for you.

**1. TOPIC SENTENCE:** *Shopping for clothes can be time consuming.*

It's best to go to a lot of stores to get an idea of the price range and quality of the clothes in each one. Of course, you have to try on many clothes to see which ones fit you best and look good on you. Some people get so tired of this process that they grab the first thing they see and buy it.

**2. *TOPIC SENTENCE:***

He has been acting up in class and disturbing the other students. We sent him to the principal's office several times, but it didn't seem to do any good. Maybe you should have a talk with him.

**3. *TOPIC SENTENCE:***

First her husband disappeared for a few days and said when he came back that he had been visiting friends in another state. Then he was away for a whole week, later claiming that the police were chasing him. But when she found the love letters, she finally believed what her friends had told her.

**4. *TOPIC SENTENCE:***

For instance, if you don't swim very well, then don't get into the water when no lifeguards are on the beach. Also, pay attention to signs that say "No Diving," since they usually signal dangerous rocks below the surface of the water.

# MATCHING TOPIC SENTENCES WITH PARAGRAPHS

Within a paragraph, the sentences that follow the topic sentence support the <u>main idea</u> expressed in that sentence. The supporting sentences might tell <u>reasons why</u> the topic sentence is true, <u>give examples</u>, or present <u>specific information</u> on the topic.

All of the paragraphs below concern one topic—voting—but each paragraph says something different about the topic. Read the paragraphs carefully and match each topic sentence to the paragraph it belongs in. Hints are provided to help you understand how topic sentences lay the basis for supporting ideas.

**A.** It's easy to register to vote.

    (*Hint: The rest of the paragraph will tell you how easy it is to register.*)

**PARAGRAPH NUMBER**_____

**B.** Voters can register in various places.

    (*Hint: The rest of the paragraph will tell you where voters can register.*)

**PARAGRAPH NUMBER**_____

**C.** Voting is optional in the United States, but this is not the case everywhere in the world.

    (*Hint: The rest of the paragraph will mention how voting works in other countries.*)

**PARAGRAPH NUMBER**_____

**1.** For example, in some parts of Latin America, failure to vote is illegal. On Election Day, officials put a stamp on the national identification cards of citizens who have voted. Those people who are later stopped by the police and don't have the stamp on their cards may be taken to prison.

**2.** The most traditional site is City Hall. In some cities you can register at libraries, too. Also, some community organizations run their own registration tables in grocery stores, at street fairs, and in other public places.

**3.** One benefit is that you participate in choosing an elected official to represent your interests. Another benefit is that you get a chance to voice your opinion, even if your candidate doesn't win.

***CONTINUED***

**D.** Even if you have voted before, you may need to register again.

(*Hint: The rest of the paragraph will tell you under what conditions you should re-register.*)

**PARAGRAPH NUMBER**_____

**E.** The biggest question in most people's minds is: Why should I bother to vote?

(*Hint: The paragraph will tell you reasons why you should vote.*)

**PARAGRAPH NUMBER**_____

*THE ANSWER KEY IS ON PAGES 88-89.*

**4.** All you need to do is show two pieces of identification, one with your current address, to the registrar. The only other thing that's required is to fill out and sign several forms.

**5.** If you move to another state, or even to another city, you may have to reregister. If you have lived in the same place for a long time but haven't voted in over four years, you may have to reregister if your name has been taken off the rolls.

# WRITING SUPPORTING SENTENCES

Of course, every paragraph you write needs more than a topic sentence to make it complete. After the topic sentence, you need to write <u>supporting sentences</u> that tell more about the main idea.

Practice writing supporting sentences for each topic sentence. Try to write three or four supporting sentences. The hints will help you.

**1.** Mondays at work are always very busy.
   *(Tell why they are busy. Give examples of people who are busy.)*

   _____

   _____

   _____

**2.** A dishonest person is dangerous to others.
   *(Tell why you think such a person is dangerous. Tell what kinds of things this person might do.)*

   _____

   _____

   _____

**3.** One of the ugliest things in the world is a garbage dump.
   *(Describe the dump. Tell what you see and smell.)*

   _____

   _____

   _____

**4.** Being a single parent is not easy.
   *(Tell why you think being a single parent is difficult. Give reasons why it would be easier to have a partner.)*

   _____

   _____

   _____

## EXERCISE 6.

# BRAINSTORMING FOR IDEAS

Sometimes you may have trouble coming up with ideas to put into your paragraph. You may be trying too hard to get things right even before you start writing. **Brainstorming** will help you get over this writer's block.

Brainstorming is the step in the writing process when the writer collects ideas about her topic. The writer can think, do research, ask questions—anything to get some ideas down on paper. At this point, it is not necessary to write complete sentences. Nor do you have to be completely sure that an idea is a good one. A brainstorm list is not the writer's final product.

Brainstorming can be difficult because you are not used to writing down everything that comes to mind. With practice, however, you will get used to this important step.

For two of the topic sentences below, write down all the ideas that come into your head. Don't try to weed out bad ideas yet. Just let your imagination run and jot ideas down as they come to you.

**1.** The house of my dreams is easy to describe.

**2.** I hate having a lot of debts.

**3.** Sex and violence on television are harmful to children.

**4.** It's important to know what you want out of life.

# WRITING TOPIC SENTENCES AND BRAINSTORMING

In the previous exercise, you brainstormed for ideas from topic sentences that were provided for you. Now try writing your own topic sentences and brainstorming for ideas.

First, think about the topic given in each item. Take some time to decide what you want to say about this topic. Then, write a topic sentence that states the *main idea* of what you want to write about.

Once you have your topic sentence, brainstorm for ideas that you might want to include in your writing. Jot down these ideas on a separate piece of paper. Don't worry too much about whether they are good ideas—right now it is important just to get thinking and writing. Save your brainstorm lists because you will use them in a later exercise.

**1.** working mothers

***TOPIC SENTENCE:***_____

_____

**2.** what your boss or teacher looks like

***TOPIC SENTENCE:***_____

_____

**3.** the worst thing that ever happened to you

***TOPIC SENTENCE:***_____

_____

**4.** waiting in line

***TOPIC SENTENCE:***_____

_____

**5.** a good job

***TOPIC SENTENCE:***_____

_____

## EXERCISE 8

# FINDING IRRELEVANT IDEAS

 When you brainstorm, you write down every idea that comes to mind, but you don't need to include all of these ideas in your paragraph. When your list is complete, you should take some time to cross out **irrelevant ideas.**

Irrelevant ideas are ideas that don't belong in your writing. These ideas do not belong in your paragraph because they do not relate to the main idea expressed in the topic sentence. Irrelevant ideas may confuse your reader and make it more difficult for him to understand the point you are trying to make.

 Cross out the irrelevant ideas from the brainstorm lists below. There are two irrelevant ideas in each list.

**1.** Everyone should do some sort of regular exercise.

pickup basketball            gym shoes

      walk to work

jogging                  swimming

     diet         exercise class

**2.** Driving home from a party when you're blasted is a bad idea.

control not as good        passengers might get hurt

     might hit someone

could wreck car         if you don't drive, there's no way to get home

     saw accident last week

**3.** Linda wants to join the Army because it seems like a good opportunity.

pays well         you get to see other countries

    basic training is a drag

the uniform is ugly       service to your country

    good way to get out of your home town

***THE ANSWER KEY IS ON PAGES 88-89.***

# WRITING A PARAGRAPH FROM A BRAINSTORM LIST

What does a writer do after she writes a brainstorm list and gets rid of irrelevant ideas? She puts her ideas into sentences and paragraphs. Below, notice how the writer expanded each idea on the list into a sentence. Pay attention to the way she added words and ideas to make the sentences complete and interesting.

*TOPIC SENTENCE:* Cleaning an oven is no fun at all.

grease everywhere

burnt food on racks

cleaning foam smells terrible

takes hours to do

~~cleaning kitchen floor is lousy too~~

oven never looks clean when done

*Cleaning an oven is no fun at all. You find grease everywhere, and it gets all over your hair and clothes. The cleaning foam smells terrible. The burnt food never comes off the racks. Even though the job takes hours to do, the oven never looks clean when you're finished!*

Go back to Exercise 7 and look over your own brainstorm lists. Choose two of the lists and write complete paragraphs based on them. Remember: read over the lists and cross out all the ideas that do not relate to the topic sentence you wrote. Then write a complete paragraph, including supporting sentences about the remaining ideas.

## EXERCISE 10

# WRITING A PARAGRAPH FROM A TOPIC

Now that you've learned to write a complete paragraph from a topic sentence and brainstorm list provided for you, you're ready to write complete paragraphs using your own topic sentence and list.

Choose <u>two</u> topics and write one complete paragraph about each of them. Here is a checklist to help you with your work:

- Think about what you want to say about the topic and write a topic sentence.
- Brainstorm for ideas. Write down everything that comes to mind about your topic sentence.
- Read over your brainstorm list and cross the irrelevant ideas off your list, leaving only those that support your topic sentence.
- Now write your paragraph, using the ideas on your list to write supporting sentences.

**1.** police protection in your neighborhood

**2.** making your own clothes

**3.** your favorite singer or musician

**4.** test tube babies

**5.** the company you work for

**6.** growing older

**7.** playing video games

**8.** being hungry

# ANALYZING A LONGER PIECE OF WRITING

Sometimes you will have so many ideas about a topic that they won't all fit into one paragraph. Longer pieces of writing usually have these parts:

- introductory paragraph
- body paragraph(s)
- concluding paragraph

An **introductory paragraph** introduces the topic and lets the reader know what will follow in the body paragraphs. The introductory paragraph contains a unifying statement that sums up the writer's message. The unifying statement tells, in a nutshell, what the topic is and what the writer plans to say about it.

The **body** of a longer piece of writing is everything between the introduction and the conclusion. The number of paragraphs in the body depends on how many ideas you want to discuss. You can write as many paragraphs as you need to make your unifying statement clear. The body paragraph(s) should support the ideas in the introductory paragraph.

A **concluding paragraph** comes at the end of a longer piece of writing. It restates the unifying idea from the introduction and summarizes the ideas developed in the body. The concluding paragraph can also present solutions for a problem discussed in the piece of writing, bring up questions, or draw conclusions.

In short, this is what you do when writing a longer piece:

- Tell your readers what you're going to tell them *(introduction)*.
- Tell them *(body)*.
- Tell them what you told them *(conclusion)*.

Read each group of paragraphs below. All of the paragraphs within each group are part of a longer piece of writing, but the paragraphs are not in order. Identify the introductory, body, and concluding paragraphs in each group. Write *I* for introductory, *B* for body, and *C* for concluding.

**1.** Earl is very fussy about what he eats, so you can let him have whatever he wants. Janette likes to stay up late, so just wait until she falls asleep and then carry her into the bedroom. Since Tony loves to watch TV, you can leave him in front of it all day long. _____

*CONTINUED*

Thanks so much for offering to take care of the kids while Bill and I are out of town. I want to let you know how we treat our children. If you follow our example, things should go smoothly. _____

Good luck. Call me if you have any problems. The phone number at my parents' house is (212) 987-1342. We'll be back on Friday. _____

**2.** To help solve this problem, I propose that we build a center for our youth. The center might include a swimming pool, basketball courts, and a roller skating rink. We could also show movies there and have regular social activities. We must do this to keep our kids away from liquor and out of trouble. _____

The young people in this little town are bored stiff, and the lack of things to do around here gets kids into a lot of trouble. They start drinking at a young age because they have nothing better to do. We must solve this problem, or our children will become alcoholic adults. _____

It's not surprising to see a group of drunk fourteen-year-olds staggering down Main Street on a Saturday night. Everybody knows about the parties in the cornfields where the guys down two six-packs apiece. These kids would like to spend their time differently, but they don't have any options. _____

**3.** Companies should give up on these gimmicks and just produce the good old originals. That way we'll have more products we can depend on and fewer surprises when we open up a new box or can of something. _____

These marketing mistakes are made all the time. I remember when the recipe of a well-known soft drink was changed. Despite the "improved" formula, the majority of the people who tasted it liked the old stuff better. A similar thing happened to the shampoo I used to use: it smelled just fine until the "new lemon scent" was added! _____

Many companies market "new" and "improved" products, hoping that their sales will increase. The fact is that, most of the time, the change is pointless. The products were much better <u>before</u> they were "improved"! _____

**4.** Please read this notice very carefully. It contains important information about your long-distance telephone service. _____

Please return the enclosed card and indicate your choice. If you do not tell us your preference by March 30, 1986, a company will be assigned to you at random by computer. _____

Because of restructuring in the telephone industry, we are now required to ask you which long-distance service you would like. The companies now offering this service are listed below. If you need more information before making a decision, you may contact any company directly. _____

**THE ANSWER KEY IS ON PAGES 88-89.**

# GROUPING WORDS AND IDEAS

An outline helps you plan the structure of a longer piece of writing. An important step in writing an outline is to categorize, or group, your ideas.

Organizing your ideas in groups helps you to organize your thoughts. It also helps you to put your ideas in a form that your reader can understand easily. Practicing grouping ideas will prepare you to write an effective outline.

Below is a list of words. Notice that all the words have one thing in common—they are all famous people. However, if you look more closely, you will see that some of these people have other things in common. Can you tell what they are?

| | | |
|---|---|---|
| Richard Nixon | John Wayne | Pope John Paul |
| Elizabeth Taylor | Jesus | Ted Kennedy |
| Abraham Lincoln | Michael Jackson | Moses |

If you examine these names carefully, you will see that three of the people listed are religious figures, three are political figures, and three are entertainers. They are all famous people, but there are three different categories of famous people.

If you were writing an essay about these people, you might want to separate them into these different categories. Your reader would find it easier to follow that way. You would group them like this:

| **POLITICAL FIGURES** | **ENTERTAINERS** | **RELIGIOUS FIGURES** |
|---|---|---|
| Richard Nixon | Elizabeth Taylor | Jesus |
| Abraham Lincoln | Michael Jackson | Pope John Paul |
| Ted Kennedy | John Wayne | Moses |

Read over each list given on the next two pages and decide what the words or ideas have in common. Write this in the space marked "Unifying Idea."

Next, think of different categories that you can divide these words or ideas into. Write these categories on the lines labeled *"Heading 1," "Heading 2,"* and *"Heading 3."*

Finally, write each word or idea from the list under the heading it belongs.

*CONTINUED*

**1.** helicopter
jeep
yacht
station wagon
canoe
Goodyear blimp
bicycle
sailboat
airplane

*UNIFYING IDEA:* _____

*HEADING 1:* _____
_____
_____
_____

*HEADING 2:* _____
_____
_____

*HEADING 3:* _____
_____
_____
_____
_____

**2.** steak
corn
string beans
red wine
beer
hamburgers
potatoes
soda pop
meatloaf

*UNIFYING IDEA:* _____

*HEADING 1:* _____
_____
_____
_____

*HEADING 2:* _____
_____
_____
_____

*HEADING 3:* _____
_____
_____
_____

**3.** mowed lawns
operated forklift
was a bank teller
promoted to bank v.p.
delivered newspapers
shoveled snow
was a metal worker
was a loan officer
ran factory assembly line

UNIFYING IDEA:_____

HEADING 1:_____

_____

_____

_____

HEADING 2:_____

_____

_____

_____

HEADING 3:_____

_____

_____

_____

**4.** has held other offices
cares about our town
promises to lower taxes
will work hard for us
has good ideas to promote
    business
will get budget under control
worked in government for past
    15 years
is honest and trustworthy
had experience as mayor's
    assistant

UNIFYING IDEA:_____

HEADING 1:_____

_____

_____

_____

HEADING 2:_____

_____

_____

_____

HEADING 3:_____

_____

_____

_____

**THE ANSWER KEY IS ON PAGES 88-89.**

# EXERCISE 13

# COMPLETING OUTLINES

An **outline** is really just a more organized brainstorm list. All ideas appear in order, and no irrelevant ideas are included. In this exercise you will be given three "skeleton" outlines for longer pieces of writing. Each outline has a unifying statement at the top and a topic sentence for each paragraph.

Fill in the blanks with your ideas for supporting sentences. Check to see that each idea is relevant to the heading you put it under. If you have more ideas than the four spaces allow, simply add them on another sheet of paper. There is no correct number of ideas. The first one is started for you.

**1. *UNIFYING STATEMENT*:** <u>I have three reasons for wanting an education.</u>

    I.   I want my family to see how important education is.
       **A:** *good model for my kids*
       **B:**
       **C:**
       **D:**

    II.  It can help me get a good job.
       **A:**
       **B:**
       **C:**
       **D:**

    III. There are lots of things I want to know more about.
       **A:**
       **B:**
       **C:**
       **D:**

**2. *UNIFYING STATEMENT*:** <u>It's a good idea to learn how to use computers.</u>

    I.   Understanding computers can help you get a job.
       **A:**
       **B:**
       **C:**
       **D:**

    II.  They are great timesaving devices.
       **A:**
       **B:**
       **C:**
       **D:**

   III.  In the year 2000, more things will be done by computer than we can imagine today.
        A:
        B:
        C:
        D:

**3. *UNIFYING STATEMENT*:** <u>Children should move away from home at the age of eighteen.</u>

   I.  Children want and need more independence.
        A:
        B:
        C:
        D:

   II.  Parents have their own reasons for wanting kids to leave.
        A:
        B:
        C:
        D:

**4. *UNIFYING STATEMENT*:** <u>There are certain things to consider when buying a used car.</u>

   I.  Is the price reasonable?
        A:
        B:
        C:
        D:

   II.  Has the car been taken care of well?
        A:
        B:
        C:
        D:

   III.  Can the dealer be trusted?
        A:
        B:
        C:
        D:

***THE ANSWER KEY IS ON PAGES 88-89.***

# EXERCISE 14

# WRITING OUTLINES

Write an outline using the brainstorm list below.

- Group the ideas according to what they have in common and get rid of irrelevant ideas.
- Draw a "skeleton outline" like those in Exercise 13. The unifying statement is given to you.
- Decide on a heading or name for each group of ideas and write a topic sentence based on the heading. Put it in its place on the outline.
- Then fill in your ideas for supporting sentences.

**UNIFYING STATEMENT:** It's unfair that trash is collected so infrequently in this community.

it's depressing to look at

no garbage in front of mayor's house

lots of potholes in street

streets look like a tornado hit them

it makes us look like slobs

people could slip on litter and hurt themselves

we want to be proud of street's appearance

bad for the environment

garbage pickup is better in Salem Heights

crime problem is getting worse

kids get sick from playing near trash

wealthy suburbs are spotless

apartments here have more roaches due to trash

# WRITING AN OUTLINE FOR A TOPIC

Here's a quick review of the steps for writing an outline:

1. Write a unifying statement.
2. Make a brainstorm list.
3. Group related ideas and cross out irrelevant ideas.
4. Write the outline.
   - Write in your unifying statement at the top.
   - Write headings for each group of related ideas from the brainstorm list.
   - Write topic sentences based on the headings and write them on outline.
   - Fill in ideas for supporting sentences under the topic sentences.

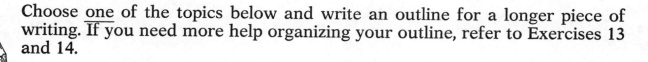

Choose <u>one</u> of the topics below and write an outline for a longer piece of writing. If you need more help organizing your outline, refer to Exercises 13 and 14.

**1.** break dancing

**2.** finding a job

**3.** adopting a child

**4.** living the good life

**5.** child abuse

**6.** television commercials

**7.** my favorite activity

**8.** nuclear weapons

**9.** pornography

# NARRATIVE WRITING

You may not realize it, but you probably already have had plenty of practice with narrating. Narrating is simply telling someone what happened or telling a story. You may have told bedtime stories to your children or younger brothers and sisters. You have probably told coworkers what you did over the weekend.

Narrative writing can be anything from a letter to a friend about your first day of work to an entry in a personal diary or journal. In this kind of writing, you may describe something or even give an opinion, but your main purpose is to tell what happened.

# BRAINSTORMING FOR NARRATIVE WRITING

Narrative pieces relate a sequence of events, give the history of something, or tell about a single incident. The unifying statement of a narrative piece should reflect your purpose. In other words, when your reader reads your unifying statement, he should know that you plan *to tell what happened.*

Once you have your unifying statement, the next step is to brainstorm. Your brainstorm list for a narrative piece will probably be just a list of events that took place. Write down these events as they come to mind.

Below is a list of topics. Choose <u>two</u> and think up a unifying statement for each one. Then write brainstorm lists based on the unifying statements you wrote.

1. an amazing coincidence

2. the first job I ever had

3. the happiest moment of my life

4. the day the world came to an end

5. the last time I moved

6. a day I would like to forget

7. a sad experience

8. my first date

# EXERCISE 2

# PUTTING THINGS IN ORDER

When you tell someone a story, you most likely start with what happened first, then second, etc. Your story is more easily understood that way. Similarly, events in a narrative paragraph are best developed in the same time order. This order is often called **sequence of events.** If you don't put the events in this order, your reader could become frustrated or completely confused.

Below are four lists of events. Put each list of events in the order in which they happened. Put a *1* next to the event that you think occurred first and a *2* next to the event that you think happened next. Continue numbering the events in each list until they are all in order.

1. _____The agency worker gave her a list of job openings.

   _____She had to get another job to support herself and her kids.

   _____She got a position as a salesclerk.

   _____She went to an employment agency.

   _____Lynnetta was laid off from her job at the shoe factory.

2. _____He came across the U.S. border in the middle of the night.

   _____His mother told him to go to the U.S. and get a job.

   _____For three months, he worked on a farm in California.

   _____Now Juan works as a busboy in Los Angeles.

   _____Juan used to live in Mexico City.

3. _____She heard a car alarm going off.

   _____Marlene woke up suddenly.

   _____A man yelled, "Get away from my car!"

   _____Marlene went back to bed and tried to fall asleep.

   _____From her window, she saw three teenagers running away.

4. _____He scanned the newspaper ads.

   _____Cory's landlord told him that his building was being sold and that he would have to leave.

   _____He answered six different ads but couldn't find anything.

   _____Cory's brother asked him to live with him, and the problem was solved.

   _____Cory began looking around for another apartment.

*THE ANSWER KEY IS ON PAGES 88-89.*

# USING TRANSITION WORDS

 Writers use **transition words** between sentences and paragraphs to make their stories easier to follow. Transitions in narrative paragraphs are usually time order words and phrases that help indicate when something took place.

Choose <u>two</u> lists you reordered in Exercise 2 and turn each one into a paragraph. Use transition words to help your reader understand the order in which things happened. The chart below provides transition words that you can use to show the sequence of events.

| | | |
|---|---|---|
| later | before | an hour earlier |
| after | as soon as | next |
| at once | last | first, second, etc. |
| meanwhile | while | as long as |
| when | until | at the same time |
| then | finally | during the morning |
| for a minute | today, tomorrow, last night | |

Remember that there is more than one way to write each paragraph. The first one is done for you.

**PARAGRAPH:** *One day, Lynnetta was laid off from her job at the shoe factory. She had to get another job to support herself and her kids. When she went to an employment agency, the agency worker gave her a list of job openings. Finally, she got a position as a sales clerk.*

**PARAGRAPH:**

## EXERCISE 4

# TELLING ABOUT YOUR DREAM

Think about a dream that you had recently or one that you had as a child that you never forgot. You can probably remember a lot of things that happened. Perhaps a monster was chasing you, or your best friend had magical powers and made her problems disappear, or you came to work one day and were told that someone else had taken over your job.

Write a narrative piece based on a dream you had. First, brainstorm—jot down everything you can remember about the dream. Next, choose the events that you think are the most important to include for your reader. Then, write a narrative piece about your dream, using transition words to make ideas clear to the reader.

When you're done, make sure that all of the sentences within each paragraph relate to the topic sentence of that paragraph.

_____

_____

_____

_____

_____

_____

_____

_____

_____

_____

_____

_____

_____

_____

_____

_____

# WRITING A SHORT STORY

Sometimes it's difficult to start writing a short story. You're not sure what or whom to write about, or you can't think of how to get an idea for a plot. The quotations below should help you get started.

Pick one of the quotations and use it in a story. The quotation can appear anywhere in your writing—at the beginning, in the middle, or at the end. Your story can take many forms: a straight narrative, a conversation, etc. Try to write at least three paragraphs.

1. "How can you do this to me?"

2. "If I never see him again, it'll be too soon for me."

3. "I never expected anything like this."

4. "Why didn't you tell me?"

5. "And to this day no one stays in that house more than a day."

6. "Listen, have I ever lied to you before?"

7. "We couldn't stop laughing."

_____

_____

_____

_____

_____

_____

_____

_____

_____

_____

_____

_____

**EXERCISE 6**

# WRITING A NEWSPAPER STORY

 When a journalist writes a story, he has to be sure that he reports the events in the order in which they happened. If he doesn't, the reader may get confused. Even worse, the people in the story may get angry because changing the order of the events might well change the meaning of the story.

 Choose <u>one</u> of the headlines below and write a newspaper story based on it. Be as specific as possible when you tell what happened, but be careful not to include irrelevant events. When you are finished, check to see that you told about all the events in the order in which they happened and that you used transition words to show the time order of the events.

*CHILDREN JUMP FROM SECOND STORY TO ESCAPE FIRE*

*HOSTAGES RELEASED AFTER 7 DAYS IN AIRPORT*

*GOVERNOR'S MISTRESS TELLS HER STORY*

*PLANE CRASHES IN PACIFIC*

*DOCTORS DISCOVER CURE FOR COMMON COLD*

*FAMOUS PAINTING STOLEN FROM NEW YORK MUSEUM*

*ROCK STAR DONATES MILLIONS TO CHARITY*

_____

_____

_____

_____

_____

_____

_____

_____

_____

_____

# NARRATING AN ACTION IN SLOW MOTION

Imagine describing an action in slow motion to someone who couldn't see you. You would soon find out that each action has many little parts that you don't notice at first.

For example, you can't describe a man washing his face just by saying that he puts soap on his face and rinses it off. The slow-motion description might go like this:

> 'He turns on the water, then plays with the faucet until he gets the right temperature. Next he picks up the bar of soap, works up a good lather, puts down the bar of soap, and rubs the lather onto his face with his hands. Then he splashes water on his face to get the soap off, grabs a clean towel, and finally puts the towel to his skin and pats his face dry.

Choose <u>one</u> of the actions below and describe it happening in slow motion. Go step by step to be sure to get all the events in order. Include as many details as you can think of and be as precise as you can. Try to use a variety of verbs so that your narration doesn't get boring.

**1.** braiding hair          **5.** eating watermelon

**2.** opening a beer can     **6.** kissing someone

**3.** brushing your teeth    **7.** shaking hands with a friend

**4.** buying a newspaper     **8.** starting a car

_____

_____

_____

_____

_____

_____

## EXERCISE 8

# WRITING A NARRATIVE ESSAY

Choose <u>one</u> of the topics below and write a three- or four-paragraph narrative piece on it. These steps will help guide you.

- Write a unifying statement that sums up your experience.
- Make a brainstorm list. Think about the experience and write down all the ideas that come to mind.
- Read over your brainstorm list and decide which events you want to include. Cross out those you want to leave out.
- Organize the events in the order in which they happened.
- Write the narrative piece, using transition words to help the reader follow the action.

1. Have you ever had a really bad day when everything went wrong? Almost everyone has.

   Tell about why that day was such a bad one.

2. How did you meet your husband/wife/girlfriend/boyfriend? Almost everyone has a story to tell.

   Tell about where and when you met and who introduced you (if someone did). Explain what fascinated you about the person at first. Tell what happened.

3. Have you ever been in a tornado, hurricane, flood, or bad snowstorm?

   Tell about what happened before, during, and after the storm. Tell how you felt about it.

4. Have you ever done something that you really regretted?

   Tell what you did. Tell the events that led up to it and what happened afterward.

5. Were you a sneaky little kid?

   Many of us were. If you were one too, tell about a trick you played on a younger brother or sister.

# NARRATIVE WRITING IN A TEST SITUATION

In this section, you have learned a lot about narrative writing. All of what you learned will be useful as you write a narrative essay for a test. This activity will give you some additional hints that can help you succeed. Also refer to the section on test essay writing starting on page 72 for more information.

The main purpose of this kind of essay test is always to <u>tell what happened</u>. In some cases, you'll be asked to choose something that happened to you and write about it. The essay question could ask you to tell about something that upset you, something that influenced your life, something that you enjoy doing, or other such events. Although the main purpose is to tell the story, you may also be asked to tell what this event means to you or why it was important.

**TEST HINTS**

- Since you will not have a great deal of time in this situation, try to decide as quickly as possible what you will write about. Try to choose a specific event that you feel strongly about so that you will have plenty, but not too much, to write about. Remember: spending a long time choosing your topic leaves you less time to organize and write.

- Remember the checklist from Exercise 8. This includes all the important elements of strong narrative writing. As you write, try to remind yourself of these points and check to be sure you are including them.

- <u>Always</u> leave at least a few minutes at the end to read over your paper. Make sure you have answered the question and try to fix as many grammar and spelling errors as you can in the time left.

In this exercise, allow yourself thirty minutes to write on the topic given below. You may not use any books. Try to keep in mind the hints given above.

> Think of an event that you feel really taught you something. It could be something that happened to you or something that happened somewhere in the world that you know about. Write an essay telling what happened and what you learned from this event.

# *PERSUASIVE WRITING*

Have you ever been asked for your opinion on an issue? Giving an opinion is simply telling someone what you think. Perhaps you have told a friend to go see a movie you enjoyed. Or maybe you told your supervisor that you thought you deserved a raise. Both of these situations are examples of giving an opinion. Giving opinions, or stating your point of view, is a big part of persuasive writing.

There is more to persuading than just stating an opinion, however. When you tell a friend to see a movie, you give her reasons to do it. When you ask your boss for a raise, you give her reasons why she should. Giving reasons that support your opinion is the other important characteristic of persuasive writing.

In the exercises that follow, you will get plenty of practice in writing your opinions and giving reasons. With all of them, remember that your purpose is *to persuade*.

# OPINIONS THAT FOCUS YOUR WRITING

Stating your point of view, or opinion, is one of the most important things in persuasive writing. If you don't know and state your opinion, the rest of the piece of writing will be unorganized and unclear.

Usually, it is a good idea to make your opinion the topic sentence of your first paragraph. In this way, your reader will know right away what your purpose and point of view are.

The writer of the paragraphs below did not state his opinion clearly. Read the reasons he gives and decide what his point of view must be. Write in this opinion as the topic sentence of the paragraph.

**1.** _____

_____

For example, spaghetti takes only a few minutes to boil, and you can buy great sauces in a jar or can. In addition, Italian food is easy because you usually have all the ingredients on hand. Chinese food, on the other hand, is difficult and time-consuming no matter what you choose to make. You have to spend hours chopping and slicing vegetables and meat. In addition, you usually end up having to run out to buy special spices or ingredients that you've never even heard of.

**2.** _____

_____

We already have over fifty jails and prisons in our state. Statistics show that putting more people in jail does not reduce the crime rate at all. Instead, the crime rate has been rising each year with each new jail we build. Furthermore, look at how much it is costing the taxpayers of this state to build these things! Let's put our money to better use.

**3.** _____

_____

I have worked in this position for over two years now. Although I enjoy the job, I feel that I need more responsibility. The position in customer service sounds interesting, and I feel I can do the job well. I don't care that there is no increase in salary; I am more interested in moving ahead in the company.

***CONTINUED***

**4.** _____

_____

For example, you never have to worry about someone stealing an old, beat-up car. However, you can be sure that a brand-new sports car will not last long unattended. In addition, you won't feel badly if your old 1970 station wagon gets a few nicks and dents, but these flaws in a new car would ruin its resale value.

**5.** _____

_____

Young people need this experience in the working world so that they learn the value of working hard for a decent wage. If we raised the minimum age to seventeen, all the fifteen- and sixteen-year-olds would be out in the street with nothing to do. With this head start into crime and laziness, they will surely become unemployed adults one day. The youth of today should have the right to work wherever and whenever they choose.

**6.** _____

_____

These people have made our world what it is today, and we need to give them credit for this. Instead of just leaving them in nursing homes and hospitals, we should make them part of our living community. The elderly have many good things still to offer. Let's take advantage of this.

**7.** _____

_____

First of all, she cried for an hour after you left. Then she proceeded to throw all her toys around the house. I had to pick up after her all night. To top it all off, she refused to go to bed at her regular bedtime. If you want me to care for your daughter again, you'll have to teach her how to behave!

**EXERCISE 2**

# PRACTICE STATING YOUR POINT OF VIEW

In class and on essay tests, you may sometimes be asked for your opinion on a given issue. You will be called on to write an essay supporting that point of view.

Sometimes you may be presented with an issue you have no opinion about. You may find that you have never considered the issue before. After thinking about it for a while, you may still not have a clear idea one way or another. In a situation like this, it is wise to choose an opinion anyway. If you do not, your essay will be incomplete and unclear to the reader.

In this exercise, practice stating opinions. For those that you really do feel strongly about, go ahead and express your opinion. For those that you are unsure of or don't particularly care about, practice choosing a side anyway. Remember that in a real essay situation, you would have to support your point of view. Make sure you state your opinions in complete sentences.

**1.** Should men and women be forced to retire at age sixty-five?

_____

_____

**2.** Reggie has been offered a promotion with his company. However, if he takes the job, he and his family will have to move to a different state, away from friends and relatives. Reggie's wife will have to quit a job she enjoys, and the children will leave a school they are happy in. Although Reggie's family comes first for him, he would like the promotion, and the family very much needs the extra money he would receive from the new job.

Should Reggie take the job or stay at his present job?

_____

_____

**3.** Do you think it's a good idea to send people who fail to file income tax reports to jail?

_____

_____

*CONTINUED*

**4.** Dexter lives in a state with a mandatory seat belt law. All drivers are required to wear a seat belt when the car is moving. One evening, Dexter was driving without his seat belt fastened. His car was struck by a drunken driver, and Dexter was paralyzed from the waist down. Dexter decided to sue the other driver.

The lawyer defending the drunk driver says that Dexter was partially to blame for his injury because he was not wearing a seat belt. He says that Dexter should receive only half of what he requested. The lawyer prosecuting the drunk driver says that the danger to society comes not from people who forget to fasten their seat belts, but from people who drink and drive. Therefore, he says, Dexter should not be penalized and should get the full amount he deserves.

Should the judge and jury award Dexter all or half of what he requested?

_____

_____


**5.** What do you think the American government should do about the problem of increasing crime in our country? Should stiffer laws and penalties be imposed to keep people from committing crime? Or should the government set up more programs to assist the unemployed and the poor? What do you think the best answer is?

_____

_____


**6.** What aspect of our country or its people should Americans be most proud of? Some people think that the physical beauty of the land is the country's finest feature. Others think we should be most proud of our contributions to world peace. What do you think?

_____

_____

# SUPPORTING YOUR OPINION

No matter how strongly and clearly you state your opinion in a persuasive paper, your reader will not be convinced unless you give him plenty of reasons to believe you. You have to be specific when you tell why you think your opinion is the right one.

In each item below, underline the word or phrase that expresses your opinion. Next, brainstorm for reasons someone should agree with you. Use the space provided to jot down your ideas. You do not have to worry about writing complete sentences.

**1.** People *(should, should not)* have to do a minimum of one hour of volunteer work per week.

**2.** Our government *(is, is not)* the strongest in the world.

**3.** Executives of large corporations *(do, do not)* make way too much money.

**4.** There *(is, is not)* more good than evil in the world today.

# WRITING PERSUASIVELY

Choose <u>one</u> of the topics from Exercise 3 and write a persuasive piece defending your position. Be sure to give good reasons to make your reader agree with you.

**EXERCISE 5**

# MAKING SURE YOUR REASONS ARE GOOD ONES

 Writers should always check to be sure they are giving strong, supportive reasons for their point of view. For example, do you think this writer gives a good reason for his opinion?

Basketball is the best sport because it is better than any other.

Saying that something is the best is the same thing as saying something is better than any other. Therefore, there is no real reason given here. The writer simply restated his opinion in a different way.

Now look at the example below and decide whether the writer is convincing.

We should vote to tear down the old building because it is a good idea.

Do you find yourself asking <u>why</u> it is a good idea? This writer was not specific in her reason, and she is therefore not convincing. Instead, she should specify <u>why</u> it is a good idea. Here is a stronger argument.

We should vote to tear down the old building because it is an ugly sight and a fire hazard.

Now you see two good reasons for tearing the building down.

In this exercise, practice *being specific* in your reasons. Replace each vague reason below with a strong, specific one of your own. If the reason given is a good one, write *supportive* on the line given.

**1.** Everyone should practice his right to vote because it is good to do so.

_____

_____

**2.** I can't stand waiting in lines since it is really annoying.

_____

_____

**3.** Women should get equal pay for equal work because they should have this right.

_____

_____

**4.** People should report crime in their neighborhood because it will help to keep the streets safer.

_____

_____

**5.** Honesty is the most important part of a relationship since it is a quality we all should have.

_____

_____

**6.** Sandy prefers studying history over doing math problems because she likes learning about people.

_____

_____

**7.** Truck drivers should get paid more than clerical workers because they deserve it.

_____

_____

**8.** Small farms in the United States are becoming obsolete because there are fewer and fewer of them.

_____

_____

**9.** It is time to look for a new apartment because our present one is too small.

_____

_____

## EXERCISE 6

# WRITING A LETTER TO THE EDITOR

In most newspapers and magazines, there is a column in which letters from readers appear. These letters can be about anything—any issue, concern, or argument that a reader wants to express. In most cases, these letters represent *persuasive* writing. The reader writes to the newspaper or magazine to express his opinion about something.

In this exercise, practice writing a letter to the editor. Choose one of the topics below and write a short letter that expresses and supports your opinion on the issue.

**1.** the traffic lights on a busy corner in your town or city

**2.** the need for more policemen

**3.** your favorite sports team

**4.** the president's economic policy

**5.** tearing down historic buildings near your home

**6.** the salaries of professional athletes

**7.** the cost of health care

**8.** racial unrest in a neighborhood

_____

_____

_____

_____

_____

_____

_____

_____

_____

_____

_____

_____

_____

# KNOWING YOUR OPPOSITION

There are different ways to be more persuasive in your arguments. You already saw that one way is to state your opinion clearly. You also saw that you should give strong and specific reasons. Another way to be sure you are being convincing is to be aware of the other point of view.

Suppose you think that building more nuclear weapons is a bad idea. You can think of ten good reasons for your opinion. To be even more persuasive, however, you need to find out why some people think building more nuclear weapons is a good idea. The more you know about your opposition's point of view, the better you will be able to convince him of your own opinion.

In this exercise, you will practice taking a stand on each side of an issue. For each statement given, brainstorm for a list of reasons. You may notice that you can come up with more ideas for one side than the other. That's OK. It probably means that you agree with one opinion more than another.

**1.** The national speed limit should be reduced to fifty miles per hour.


The national speed limit should not be reduced to fifty miles per hour.


**2.** As a nation, we do little to help the poor and homeless.


As a nation, we do a lot to help the poor and homeless.


**3.** Teachers get paid too much money for the job they do.


Teachers don't get paid enough money for the job they do.

## EXERCISE 8

# OVERCOMING THE OPPOSITION

Once you know some of the reasons that your opponent disagrees with you, you can use them to your advantage. In your argument, you can try to prove why her reasons are not good ones.

For example, as in Exercise 7, you want to write about why building more nuclear weapons is a bad idea. You jot down some of your reasons. Then, you think about why someone might disagree with you. Perhaps you come up with an argument like this:

> We should build more nuclear weapons because we need protection from other nations with nuclear arms.

To persuade this person that your point of view is a better one, you will have to address her concern. Therefore, in your piece of writing, you might write:

> Building more nuclear weapons does not protect us from the threat of a nuclear attack from another nation. It only encourages them to increase their numbers as well.

Perhaps your reader will not be convinced, but addressing her concern directly is better than completely ignoring it.

In this exercise, choose <u>one pair</u> of brainstorm lists from Exercise 7. Choose the side you are most comfortable with and write an essay defending this position. The "opposition's" brainstorm list will help you see what <u>specific</u> arguments you will have to overcome.

_____

_____

_____

_____

_____

_____

_____

_____

_____

_____

# WRITING ADVICE COLUMNS

One common kind of persuasive writing is one that gives advice to someone. You may be familiar with "Dear Abby" letters in the newspaper. People write in with problems or questions, and the letters and responses are printed in a special column of the paper.

Imagine that you are "Abby." You have received the following letters to respond to in your column. Choose <u>two</u> of them and write a short letter giving advice.

**1.** Dear Abby:

My boyfriend is always bugging me to get married. I like him a lot, but I'm not interested in marriage. We have been together for over five years, and he is getting angrier and angrier with me. I want to be with him, but I don't think I will ever want to get married—to him or anyone else. What should I do?

Knows Better

**2.** Dear Abby:

My problem is my wife and her lack of understanding. After working hard all week, I like to go out with my buddies on Friday nights—<u>no women allowed.</u> My wife thinks that I should be spending every night of the weekend at home with her. Can I help it if she has no friends of her own? Abby, how can I make her understand that this setup really helps our marriage? Or am I being unreasonable?

Thank God for
Fridays

**3.** Dear Abby:

What is a good way to get guests to leave your home when you want them to? I have three or four friends who come over a couple times a week to play cards or watch a movie. When we are finished, usually around midnight, they like to sit around and talk. I would rather go to bed so I can get up on time for work.

Abby, the last time I asked a friend to leave my house, she never came back again! I don't want to lose my friends, but I need some rest.

Haggard Host

# PERSUADING IN ADVERTISEMENTS

Another very common example of persuasive writing is <u>advertising</u>. Companies and organizations attempt to <u>persuade</u> you to buy or do something. One ad might tell you all the health benefits you'll get from eating a certain cereal. Another ad might urge you to donate money to a senior citizens' organization. Both of these are examples of persuasive writing.

Open a magazine or newspaper and look closely at some of the advertisements. What techniques do they use to persuade the reader? Notice the specific reasons they give. Also notice the appealing describing words they use. Then, notice how the ad can be directed at a specific audience, such as a mother or an athlete. Look carefully at how the ad writer uses specific reasons to persuade that audience. As you can see, when you write an advertisement, you use many of the techniques you have already learned about in persuasive writing.

In this exercise, write an advertisement for <u>one</u> of the items below. Since all the items listed are very common, you will really have to use your imagination. Make sure your ad is directed at a particular audience and be as persuasive as possible.

**1.** a used toothbrush

**2.** a fork

**3.** lined paper

**4.** purple hair ribbon

**5.** book of matches

**6.** dirty wastebasket

**7.** single sock

**8.** a small screwdriver

# WRITING AN ADVERTISEMENT

Suppose you could "manufacture" human qualities, such as honesty, anger, sympathy, and love. You are able to sell these qualities at a very low cost to people who do not have such qualities.

Choose one human quality and write an advertisement for it. Give specific reasons why someone would want and enjoy it. Remember, your audience is someone who does not have this quality.

# PERSUASIVE WRITING IN THE TEST SITUATION

Much of what you have learned in this section will help you prepare for taking a persuasive essay test. Here are some hints to keep in mind as well. For more information on taking an essay test, turn to page 72.

**TEST HINTS**
- Be sure that you understand the essay question.
- Remember to choose one point of view and state it clearly in your introductory paragraph.
- Support your position with specific reasons and examples.

Choose <u>one</u> of the following situations and write a persuasive essay for it. Give yourself thirty minutes to plan and write. You may not use any books, just as if you were taking a real essay test. Remember to state your position clearly and to brainstorm to come up with strong, supportive reasons. Also keep your audience in mind and try to overcome their objections.

1. Your friend is depressed about his/her family life. He or she is not getting along with his/her spouse and is considering getting a divorce. You want to cheer your friend up, but you also want to give some advice. Write a letter to this friend.

2. You feel that you deserve a raise in your present job. Your supervisor has asked you to give your proposal in writing. She says that the company is going through some difficult times and that they have little money for raises. You still feel you deserve one. Write a letter telling your supervisor why you should get a raise.

3. You read an article in your newspaper about a woman who shot and seriously wounded a man who tried to grab her purse. The article stated that the woman "sensed" that she was in danger, but suffered no harm. You decide that you'd like to write a letter to the editor to share your opinion on this situation.

4. News reports over the past several years have informed us that the young adult suicide rate is on the rise. More and more of our young people, overcome with loneliness, peer pressure, and a sense of being "lost," feel that death is the only escape.

   Explain why young people commit suicide. Be sure to support your views with specific reasons, details, and examples.

# DESCRIPTIVE WRITING

Descriptive writing is writing that shows while it tells. Think of going to a movie. You see a picture on the screen, hear the words and music and other sounds all at the same time. Descriptive writing is similar to a movie but is often much more. It can include all of your senses: seeing, smelling, tasting, touching, and hearing. Descriptive writing often includes emotions and thoughts as well. You describe a scene that comes alive again as you tell and write about it.

The following exercises will help you to practice using your senses, thoughts, and emotions to describe situations to someone else. If you make your written picture clear and specific enough so that your audience can "see" it in their own imaginations, you will have found an effective and enjoyable means of communication.

# BRAINSTORMING

Descriptive writing, like all writing, needs to start somewhere. Getting started is often the most difficult part of the entire process. You may feel like you have thousands of ideas clashing with each other in your mind's eye, or maybe you have none at all. Sometimes you feel like you're lost in a brainstorm.

As you know, *brainstorm* also has another meaning. It can be an activity to help you get started. Think of the people, places, and things that attract your attention, for whatever reasons; they could be good or bad, serious or funny. No matter what the reason, you should feel strongly about the subject.

Look at the chart below. Under each heading ("People," "Places," "Things"), make a list of possible things to describe. Underneath each person, place, or thing, briefly state your reason for listing it. Look at the examples for ideas. Your reasons may be a single word or many.

| PEOPLE | PLACES | THINGS |
|---|---|---|
| 1. *Jack* | *job* | *baseball glove* |
| *fixed the fridge* | *machine crushed Bill* | *Nancy lost new one* |
| 2. | | |
| 3. | | |
| 4. | | |
| 5. | | |
| 6. | | |

# EXERCISE 2

# CHOOSING AND LISTING

Often, you must make quick choices during the writing process. You have to choose what to write about or choose which ideas to include and which to leave out. Sometimes the choices are made for you. Sometimes you feel as if the words have selected themselves. Look over the three lists you made in Exercise 1. Which of the items seem to stand out from all of the others? Which seem to select you? Which do you feel most strongly about? Which can you see in your own mind?

Choose one item from each category in Exercise 1 ("People," "Places," "Things") and circle it with your pen or pencil. Write each item and the reason you chose it on the lines at the top of the chart below. Then brainstorm again. Under each heading, list everything that has to do with the items. Be as specific as possible. Remember: you don't have to worry about what is a "good" idea and what isn't. Just write whatever comes to mind.

**PERSON**
*ITEM:*


*REASON:*


**PLACE**
*ITEM:*


*REASON:*


**THING**
*ITEM:*


*REASON:*


***NOTE:*** At this point, you may want to discuss the choices that you have made with your classmates and teacher. Talking things out and sharing ideas can be an important and useful part of brainstorming and writing.

## EXERCISE 3

# PUTTING THINGS IN ORDER/ CUTTING OUT THE JUNK

 Often, when you write quickly, your ideas may appear jumbled. Some of them may not belong in the piece at all; you may have to add others. Look at what you wrote in Exercise 2 and choose <u>one</u> person, place, or thing you wrote about. Do some ideas in your list seem stronger than others? Could some ideas be in a better order? In this exercise, you will use the ideas from your brainstorm list to write a description of the person, place, or thing you selected.

 First, pick out the most important ideas from your list and circle them. Cross out things that are not needed. Next, on a piece of scratch paper, add any ideas that have been omitted. Make sure to include all of the necessary tastes, smells, sights, etc., that will really help your readers experience what you want them to. Don't forget to put down what you think and feel.

Now use these ideas to write your description. Try to write at least two paragraphs.

_____

_____

_____

_____

_____

_____

_____

_____

_____

_____

_____

_____

_____

_____

_____

## EXERCISE 4

# EVERYTHING HAPPENS IN A PLACE/USING YOUR SENSES

 William Shakespeare and a few other people have said that "all the world is a stage." Everything happens somewhere—in a place. What place (where something happens) is most important to you? Can you see that place as a "stage" where your description is like a movie scene, playing itself out? What is the main action going on in the place? See the place in your imagination. "Look" at it as you answer the following questions. When you are finished answering the questions, use your ideas to write a paragraph or two describing this place.

What is the key action in the center of the place?

_____
_____
_____

What people are involved in the action?

_____
_____
_____

What are they saying to each other?

_____
_____
_____

What are their hands doing?

_____
_____
_____

Where do they move around in the place?

_____
_____
_____

What objects are they using?

_____

_____

_____

What sounds can be heard in the place? What does the place smell like?

_____

_____

_____

What are some of the textures (things that you can actually feel with your fingertips) in the place?

_____

_____

_____

What is the weather like? (There is "weather" even inside).

_____

_____

_____

**PARAGRAPH:**_____

_____

_____

_____

_____

_____

_____

_____

_____

## EXERCISE 5

# BEING SPECIFIC

As you probably realize, writers need to use specific details in their descriptions. If they don't, their readers may not clearly "see" what is being described. A word like *small*, for example, might need to be explained further. Your idea of "small" may be different from someone else's. A reader might think of "small" as the size of a mouse. You, on the other hand, might see "small" as the size of a safety pin. If you want your reader to "see" the picture you see, you need to <u>be specific.</u>

We also use specific images to <u>show</u> our readers what we mean. Can you get a good idea of what is happening in the sentence below? Is this a very descriptive sentence?

> Veronica was very happy.

How do we know Veronica was happy? What did she do? How did she show she was happy? Here is a descriptive sentence that <u>shows</u> rather than <u>tells</u>.

> Veronica's smile looked as if it would never leave her face.

Being specific and showing rather than telling your reader are two good ways to be more descriptive in your writing.

In this exercise, read each sentence and try to get a picture of it in your mind. Then rewrite the sentence so that it is more descriptive. Remember to be specific and to show your reader what is happening. The first one is done for you.

**1.** The man looked very nervous as he waited in line.

*The disheveled man fidgeted uneasily as he waited in line.*

**2.** The room was a real mess.

_____

**3.** Seeing a lonely child makes me sad.

_____

**4.** It was a dark evening.

_____

**5.** She is a beautiful woman.

_____

**6.** It was a big mistake.

_____

# COMPARING FOR SIMILARITIES

As we have seen, descriptive writing is writing that shows while it tells. To show something, you must be able to see it clearly yourself so that the audience can see it clearly. If you were to go on a trip and it was foggy the whole time, could you tell someone later what the place looked like?

One way to "cut through the fog" is to compare something (or someone) to something else. *Comparing* means telling what two things have in common—what makes them alike. Even different kinds of things (or people) can be compared. For example, carpenters and musicians are very different kinds of people; however, if we look, we can find similarities between them. Both groups of people use tools in their work. Both make a lot of noise when they work. Both make things that are useful and enjoyable for society. How many other similarities can you think of for carpenters and musicians?

In this exercise, choose <u>two</u> different places, things, or people. Write them on the lines given. Then, compare and see how many similarities you can find. Jot down these similarities on the lines below. Finally, write a paragraph comparing these two people, places, or things. One example is given.

*construction worker*       *ballerina*

*both use their muscles, both create something in their work*

**EXERCISE 7**

# COMPARING FOR DIFFERENCES (CONTRASTING)

There is another kind of comparing that you can do that will help you to see and describe things more clearly. You can compare <u>differences</u> between people, places and things. Comparing differences is called *contrasting*. We contrast all the time in our daily lives. If you were going to buy a new car, you would be looking for differences in color, style, power, cost, speed, etc., before you made a decision. You would certainly look at both cars closely.

On the lines below, choose two "dream cars." Contrast their differences and jot these ideas on the lines that follow. Finally, write your contrast in paragraph form.

**DREAM CAR #1** _____ **DREAM CAR #2** _____

_____

_____

_____

_____

**PARAGRAPH:** _____

_____

_____

_____

_____

_____

_____

_____

_____

# ADDING DETAILS

He came over to my house the other night and picked me up. We hung around awhile, and then we did some stuff. After that we went over to this other guy's place, but he wasn't home because he got in a little trouble.

Although you can probably guess that this is someone's account of how he and some friends spent an evening, you don't actually know what happened; you can't see it. If the writer used more describing words and more specific nouns and verbs, it would be clearer. It would be more descriptive. For example, look at the paragraph rewritten:

Rico blasted through the kitchen door just when we were eating supper. I could tell something was up because he was really nervous. He tried to be cool when my mom offered him something to eat, but he kept tapping his foot under the kitchen table like he was ready to bounce up and fly out of there. He was scared. His nose runs when he's scared, and he kept sniffling. Well, finally we got out of there, and we ran all the way to Stash's house over at the Square. Stash had been busted for ripping off some radios from Oly's place. We knew we'd be next.

Reread the first paragraph and rewrite it in your own words. You choose the people, the places, and the things to tell. See it happen in your own mind and tell what you see. Remember to use describing words and phrases and don't forget to be specific.

_____

_____

_____

_____

_____

_____

_____

_____

_____

# SIMILES AND METAPHORS: SPECIAL COMPARISONS THAT SHOW DETAILS

Descriptive writing needs to create a picture in our minds to be strong and successful. We have seen that when we use comparisons and contrasts we can create a clearer picture. Here's another way to use comparisons to give greater detail to a piece of writing.

**Similes** and **metaphors** are special kinds of comparisons that create pictures in our minds (images). What pictures are created in your mind when you read these similes?

His hair looked **like** a briar patch.

Her feet are **as big as** surfboards.

As you can see, similes often use the words *like* and *as.*

Metaphors work much like similes, but they involve broader comparisons than similes. Here is a metaphor that uses an image of an earthquake **to** describe a wrestler:

When Hulk Hogan entered the ring against the Bruiser, the roar that shook the auditorium was so powerful that it **could have been an earthquake:** the floors shook; the rafters creaked; and nozzles on the beer taps exploded.

Notice that both similes and metaphors use specific details to help you get a clearer picture.

Rewrite the following paragraph describing a wait in an unemployment office. Use similes (comparing with *like* or *as*) and at least one metaphor (a broader image) to make the writing clearer.

The unemployment office was large. The line was long. I had to wait a long time to see a clerk. While I waited, I saw all kinds of people. I could see anger and sadness in their faces. The most horrible thing was that many people had waited all day and then were told that they could not be seen.

# PUTTING IT ALL TOGETHER

You have written quite a lot so far and should congratulate yourself for that. As you can see, descriptive writing is not a one-shot deal. It takes time and a series of different steps to help your reader "see" what you, the writer, want him to. Your last step is to put it all together.

In this exercise, choose <u>one</u> of the topics to write a descriptive piece. Use these steps to help you remember all the features of strong descriptive writing.

- Brainstorm for all kinds of ideas to include about your topic. Jot down everything that comes to mind.

- Choose the ideas that are most important to your description and circle them. Cross out the ones that don't really belong there.

- Put your ideas into a logical order that your reader will find easy to follow.

- Write your description, using specific words and phrases that will help your reader really "see" what you are describing. Remember that descriptive writing <u>shows</u> while it tells.

1. Describe how you feel when someone lets you down.

2. Describe your most memorable childhood toy.

3. Describe how someone looks when he is angry.

4. Describe a place that you spend a lot of time in.

5. Describe an object you have in your pocket right now.

6. Describe what the word *tired* means to you.

7. Describe your idea of the perfect deserted island.

8. Describe someone who is lonely.

## EXERCISE 11

# DESCRIPTIVE WRITING IN A TEST SITUATION

In a test situation, you may be asked to describe a person, place, or thing to your reader. You have already learned a great deal about descriptive writing in this section, and all of this information and practice will help you on a test. However, here are some specific hints that can help you as you write for an essay test. In addition, refer to the test section on page 72 for more information.

**TEST HINTS**

- In many cases, you will be asked to describe the person, place, or thing of your choice. Don't spend too much time in this selection process, however. The more time you spend deciding, the less time you will have to organize and write. Try to choose something that you can visualize very clearly, as your best writing comes from images you are intimately familiar with.

- Always keep in mind that your reader cannot see what you see. Don't make the reader guess at what you mean. Remember that your idea of "big" might be a tractor trailer, but your reader might think of "big" as the city of New York. Keep your reader in mind as you write and be specific in your descriptions.

- Leave enough time to go over what you have written. Try to fill in as many gaps as you can find. Then, check for grammar and spelling errors and correct them.

In this exercise, allow yourself thirty minutes to plan and write the essay below. As in a real test situation, you may not use any books. Keep in mind the hints given above.

Think of some person, place, or thing that you have seen recently enough that you remember lots of details. It could be your father's house, the Statue of Liberty, your son or daughter, or any other person, place, or thing. Write an essay that describes it to a reader who has never seen it. Remember to use specific details.

# INFORMATIVE WRITING

We inform people when we tell them the *facts* about something. The writer provides knowledge about a topic or makes something easier to understand by explaining it. Unlike persuasive writing, informative writing does not include the writer's opinions. Informative writing sticks to the facts.

For example, when you write a note to a delivery person explaining what to do with a package, your writing is *informative*. When you write a report telling your supervisor about a meeting you attended, this report represents *informative* writing. You can find many examples of informative writing in newspapers and magazines. Except for advertisements and editorials, all writing you find there can be called informative.

Keep in mind that informative writing should be specific. In order to inform your readers effectively, you have to make sure you have included all the important information they may need to know. If you do not, your readers will be lost and you will not be as informative as you should. For example, what would happen if you wrote out invitations to a party but did not tell where it was to be held? Your readers would probably not make it because they were uninformed.

The exercises in this section will allow you to practice writing to inform. Keep your reader in mind as you write and try to be specific in your facts and ideas.

## EXERCISE 1

# IDENTIFYING THE FACTS

In order to give the reader enough information to understand, informative writing answers these questions: *Who? What? When? How? Where?* Sometimes you don't need to include the answers to all these questions, but in most cases, more information is better than less.

Read the informative paragraphs below. As you read, find the information that answers the questions that follow. Then, write this information in the space provided. Some questions will have more than one response. The first one is started for you.

1. Teenagers in the United States are becoming more and more conscious of their health than ever before. In the year 1986 alone, these young people consumed 15% more fruit than the previous year and 10% less salty snacks such as potato chips and pretzels. Health experts say that this trend is due to the increasing interest in weight control and physical fitness.

   **WHO?** *U. S. Teenagers*    **WHAT?**

   **WHEN?** *1986*    **WHERE?**

   **WHY?**

2. On July second of this year, school administrators in Franklin and Canton predicted a teacher strike in the fall. The reasons given for the possible strike include low pay, lack of job security, and poor working conditions. If an agreement is not reached by September 1, public school students from both districts will not return to school on the regularly scheduled date.

   **WHO?**    **WHAT?**

   **WHEN?**    **WHY?**

   **WHERE?**

3. Fifteen thousand protesters from anti-nuclear groups across the country marched in Washington last Wednesday. They demanded a decrease in the defense budget and the end of U.S. participation in the nuclear arms race. The event's organizers say they hope that the march will call attention to important bills now in the Senate and make more people aware of the increased threat of nuclear war.

   **WHO?**    **WHAT?**

   **WHEN?**    **WHERE?**

   **WHY?**    **HOW?**

# MAKING YOUR FACTS SPECIFIC

Without specific facts, your reader might not understand what you mean. He may get the wrong idea about something you wrote. This can lead to confusion and frustration.

When you are writing to inform, make sure you include enough detail. For example, if you want to mention an event that occurred a long time ago, it would not make sense to write down only the month and day of the event. You would want to include the year as well. Or, if you are writing a comparison of prices at different stores, simply stating that one store is more expensive than another may not convince your reader. You should probably include some specific examples of prices so that your reader can actually "see" what you are talking about. Specific details are always more informative than general facts.

In this exercise, practice giving your facts more detail. Rewrite each sentence below, but include more specific information than what is given. Answering the questions after each sentence should help you be more specific. Imagine that you have done some research to find these facts and just make them up yourself. The first one is done for you.

**1.** Sales of fruit juices are higher this year than last year.
   *(How much higher? In what years?)*

   <u>Sales for fruit juices are 20% higher in 1986 than they were</u>

   <u>in 1985.</u>

**2.** Manfred is taller than Tammy.
   *(How much taller?)*

   _____

**3.** The warehouse has lots of books left in stock.
   *(What warehouse? How many books?)*

   _____

**4.** The hole in the fence is pretty small.
   *(What fence? How small is "pretty small"?)*

   _____

**5.** It was one February when we had all that snow.
   *(Which February? How much snow?)*

   _____

**EXERCISE 3**

# GIVING DIRECTIONS

The scene is probably familiar to you. You're standing on a street corner waiting for the light to change. A car pulls up. The driver rolls down the window and shouts, "Hey, do you know how to get to Federal Savings?"

Your answer is an example of giving information: telling *how* and *where*.

In this exercise, imagine that your friends are in town for the weekend. They need you to give them directions for getting from place to place. Using the map below, write down directions for each of the items given below. You will have to be as specific as possible because your friends have never been here before and have difficulty following directions.

1. They mentioned that their car needs a tune-up. Write a paragraph telling how to <u>drive</u> to the gas station from your house. Watch out for one way streets.

2. After they meet your kids at school, they want to pick up some desserts. Write a paragraph telling them how to <u>walk</u> from Payton School to the bakery.

3. There's a good movie in town that they want to see. Write a paragraph telling how to <u>walk</u> from the bakery to the theater.

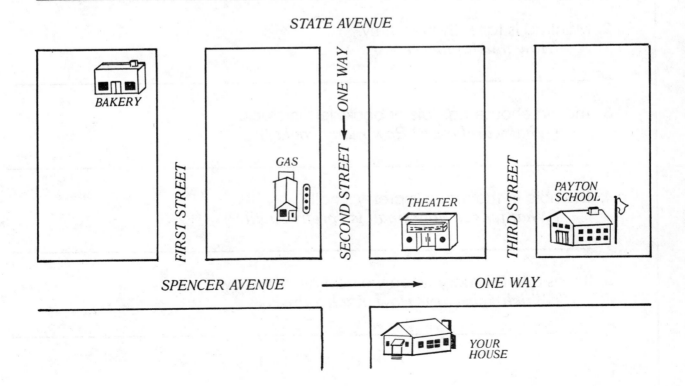

# USING FACTS TO INFORM

Sometimes you give information based on what you can remember. Other times, you may need to refer to charts, tables, graphs, and other sources when writing informative pieces. In this exercise, you will get practice doing informative writing based on a chart.

Psychologists have determined that when people undergo many stressful events, they are more likely to become ill. Below is a chart that outlines some stress factors. All of the events listed are stressful, but some events are harder to handle than others. The events are listed in order, from the hardest to the easiest to cope with.

### MOST DIFFICULT EVENTS
1. death of husband or wife
2. divorce
3. marital separation
4. being held in jail
5. major personal injury
6. getting married
7. losing a job
8. retirement

### LEAST DIFFICULT EVENTS
1. change in working hours
2. changing to a new school
3. change in social life
4. change in church
5. taking out a mortgage
6. change in sleeping habits
7. change in eating habits
8. vacation

To get some ideas for writing a paragraph based on this chart, answer these questions:

1. Some of the items on the "Most Difficult Events" list are positive. Why do you think these events are considered stressful?

   _____

2. What is similar about a lot of the items on the "Least Difficult Events" list?

   _____

3. What, if anything, do <u>all</u> the events in both lists have in common?

   _____

4. What are the differences between the two lists?

   _____

Write an informative paragraph about stressful events that can lead to illness. Use the chart and your answers to the questions to guide you.

## EXERCISE 5

# WRITING A REPORT FROM NOTES

 Imagine that you attended a workshop as part of your responsibilities at work. Your boss was unable to attend the workshop. She wants you to write a report on one of the lectures she missed.

 Below are the notes you took. Read them over and decide on a unifying statement that sums up what you want to say in your report. Cross out any ideas you don't want to include. Organize your ideas into smaller groups of related ideas. Draw up an outline and write a complete report.

- Margaret Johnson, speaker from Urban League
- originally from Philadelphia
- 20 years as prenatal class teacher
- topic: infant mortality (babies dying before they're a year old)
- 10,000 per year in U.S.
- happens to twice as many blacks as whites
- low-income mothers can't pay medical fees; don't get care before baby is born
- early prenatal care and good maternal nutrition can prevent infant mortality
- remember the four basic food groups
- results of poor nutrition and health care: babies are born too small, stillborn, handicapped
- happens more often in low-income areas
- federal spending cuts worsen problem—women can't get Medicaid anymore
- problem not as bad in most European countries (gov't pays medical expenses)
- solution: pass laws to allocate funds for new clinics in poverty-stricken areas
- more money from the gov't

# WRITING A NEWSPAPER ARTICLE

If you look in most newspaper articles, you will see that they include many facts. The writer tells specifically the *who, what, when, how,* and *where* of his subject.

Practice writing a newspaper article based on <u>one</u> of the headlines below. Remember not to leave your reader guessing— include all necessary facts and details. Answering "the 5 *W*s" in the beginning of the article will capture the reader's interest and keep him informed. Turn back to Exercise 1 if you want to review the 5 *W*s.

1. *PITCHER SAM DESMOND EARNS TENTH SHUTOUT*

2. *WEALTHY WOMAN ARRESTED FOR SHOPLIFTING*

3. *MAYOR PLANS CITY-WIDE CELEBRATION*

4. *BISHOP FIRES TOP ASSISTANT*

5. *TEENAGER WINS LOTTERY JACKPOT*

6. *PEACE COMES TO WAR-TORN NATIONS*

7. *STAR ATHLETE DIES OF DRUG OVERDOSE*

8. *POLICE CLASH WITH PROTESTERS*

_____

_____

_____

_____

_____

_____

_____

_____

_____

_____

## EXERCISE 7

# WRITING INSTRUCTIONS

Have you ever explained to someone how to do something or why something happens? If you have, you probably noticed how important it is to be specific. You need to add lots of details and include informative examples so that this person can follow the instructions clearly.

When you are actually with the person, you probably use many hand gestures and demonstrations to make your point. When something is confusing, the person can ask questions. After a while, you can probably make yourself understood.

When you write down instructions, your reader will not have the advantage of seeing hand gestures or asking questions. All your reader will have are your written words. This is what makes writing instructions tricky. The need to be specific is even greater.

In this exercise, write instructions for something you know how to do well. A list of topics is given if you are having trouble thinking of one. Remember that your reader knows nothing about your topic and has never performed this task before. Include any important details this reader will need to perform this task.

**1.** playing poker

**2.** training a dog

**3.** using a calculator to add and subtract

**4.** changing a baby's diapers

**5.** joining your club or union

**6.** writing a check

_____

_____

_____

_____

_____

_____

_____

_____

_____

_____

_____

# SLOW MOTION INSTRUCTIONS

Here is an exercise that will really stretch your ability to make your information specific.

Imagine that a creature from another planet has come down to earth and wants you to explain how to perform a very simple task. This creature can understand only <u>very specific</u> actions. For example, if you want to tell it how to open a desk drawer, it won't understand if you say, "Hold the handle and pull out." Instead, you will have to imagine that this action is taking place in <u>slow motion</u>. You would need to give it these instructions:

> Stretch out your arm as far as it will go in the direction of the drawer handle. Open your hand and place it on the handle. Bend your fingers around the handle until they are hooked completely around it. Now bend your arm while still holding on to the handle. You will see the drawer opening now. Keep bending your arm until the drawer is open as wide as you need it.

Choose a topic from those below and write instructions in slow motion that the creature will understand. Don't leave out any details!

**1.** how to wind a watch

**2.** how to pick flowers

**3.** how to do a sit-up

**4.** how to put on lipstick

**5.** how to applaud

**6.** how to pour milk

_____

_____

_____

_____

_____

_____

_____

_____

_____

# WRITING AN EXPLANATION

Sometimes on essay assignments and tests, you'll be asked to explain something. In other words, you will have to give reasons why something occurs or why someone acts as he does. In a way, you will be giving your opinion, just as you do in persuasive writing. However, this kind of essay assignment does not call on you to choose one side or another. Instead, you simply tell what you think and why.

As in all informative writing, when you explain, you must be specific. Your reasons must be "real" to your reader. For example, if your essay states that people cheat because they want to get ahead at all costs, you should include "proof" for your explanation. Perhaps you could tell a story about a student you know who cheats to get better grades. Or, if you were able to do some research, you might find statistics to back up your statement.

In this exercise, choose <u>one</u> of the following topics and write an essay on it. First brainstorm to come up with some ideas. Decide which ideas to include and get rid of the others. Write the essay and remember to be specific with your reasons and examples.

1. People are jealous for different reasons. They can be jealous of other people's possessions, looks, or status. Some people seem to be "the jealous type," while others don't even seem to notice other people.

   Write an essay that explains what makes people jealous. Why are some people jealous and others not? Be specific when you give reasons and examples.

2. Most people feel that they have "learned some lessons" in their past. They may have made some mistakes that taught them something. They may wish that they had acted differently than they did in the past.

   What is one thing you have learned from your past? What would you do differently if you could? Explain what you learned and why it is important to you. Remember to be specific.

# INFORMATIVE WRITING IN A TEST SITUATION

You have learned quite a bit about informative writing in this section. All of what you have learned can be put to good use on an essay test. However, here are some specific hints that should help you out.

**TEST HINTS**

- The most important aspect of informative writing— whether it is to explain or give instructions or directions—is being specific. Wherever you can, supply proof and examples to back up and support your ideas.

- Be sure you take a few minutes to jot down a brainstorm list before you start writing. Include steps to follow (if giving directions or instructions) or reasons for an explanation.

- Avoid vague terms and references in your writing. Some describing words mean different things to different people, so try to stick with words and phrases that have one clear meaning that can't be confused.

- Keep your explanations simple. Be sure you have a good idea why something happens or how something works before you start to explain it. Then write your explanation in simple, direct language. If things get too complicated, you will lose your reader.

In this exercise, you have thirty minutes to write on the essay topic given below. As in a real test situation, you are not allowed to use any books. Keep in mind the hints you saw above.

Most people go through periods when they feel "down" or "low." This type of depression can last as short a time as a few hours or as long as several months. It may be brought on by an incident such as a death in the family or the loss of a job. On the other hand, it can occur in otherwise happy people for no apparent reason.

What causes depression? What can be done to prevent it? What can be done about your own depression when it occurs? Be sure to support your explanation with specific reasons, details, and examples.

# WRITING IN A TEST SITUATION

More and more often, students are being asked to demonstrate their writing ability on tests. You may already be familiar with writing tests that ask you to fill in blanks or correct errors. Essay tests are different from these because you are asked to compose a piece of writing yourself in response to a question.

Writing in a test situation is a little different from the writing you do normally. Because of the time limit imposed on essay tests, you may not be able to write and revise a detailed outline. You also will not have access to a dictionary or grammar book that you may usually rely on in your everyday writing. In addition, you will be asked to write on a given topic—not one of your own choosing. All of these factors make writing in a test situation different from the writing you have done so far.

However, all the skills you have been developing in this book and other writing books will be helpful to you. You will still use the "process approach" to writing, but you will use it in a shortened form. Everything you have learned about writing strong topic sentences, using organization, being specific, etc., holds true in an essay test. Don't feel that you have to forget all you know about writing just because you are now preparing for an essay test.

The following exercises will allow you to practice writing for tests. Each activity will give you hints and guidelines that can help you get prepared for different types of writing assignments you may find in a test situation.

# READING THE QUESTION CAREFULLY

One of the most important parts of taking any test is <u>reading directions</u>. This is especially true for essay tests or in-class writing assignments. You need to know what is being asked for in order to answer the question clearly.

Some essay questions will ask you what you think about an issue or idea. Others will ask you to describe something that happened to you. Still others will ask you to write about something that you like, dislike, or hope for. You would respond to each topic in a different way.

When taking an essay test, first read carefully through the <u>stimulus</u>. The stimulus is the material you are being asked to respond to. Then, look for clue words and phrases such as "tell what happened," "describe," or "give your opinion" that can help you understand what you are being asked to do. Some questions may require you to make a choice before you begin writing. Look for phrases such as "either...or" that indicate you need to choose one thing or another. Also pay particular attention to phrases such as "give specific reasons" or "give examples." Remember that these are part of your directions.

**TEST HINT**

> After you read over an essay question, go back and reread it carefully. Then, underline words and phrases that tell you what is being asked for. As you write, refer to your underlined ideas to make sure you are on track.

In this exercise, read each essay question carefully, but <u>do not answer it</u>. Instead, briefly jot down *how* you think you should answer it. Remember to read the stimulus first and pick out clue words and phrases. The first one is done for you.

**1.** Almost everyone has had "one of *those* days" when everything seems to go wrong. This kind of day can make you both angry and frustrated. Write an essay telling what happened on a day when everything went wrong for you. Describe how you felt about it.

*Write about the day I lost my keys. Tell what happened:*

*couldn't lock up apartment, couldn't take the car to work. Tell*

*how I felt: frustrated and angry.*

**2.** Think of something that you think is unfair. It can be something you have experienced in your own life or something that you know happens

**CONTINUED**

in the world. Write an essay about this unfair thing. Tell what happened and how you feel about it.

_____

_____

_____

**3.** Do you think women should have the right to have an abortion if they so choose? Write an essay in which you give your opinion on this issue. Make sure you give specific reasons for your point of view.

_____

_____

_____

**4.** More and more people are deciding to become single parents. Unmarried men and women are applying to adopt infants and children, and adoption agencies are debating over whether this is a good idea. Should single adults be able to adopt children to raise on their own, or should agencies require both a mother and father in the home? Write an essay telling what you think and give specific details and examples.

_____

_____

_____

**5.** Think of something you would like to change about either yourself or a close friend. Write an essay telling the one quality you would change and why.

_____

_____

_____

**6.** Our president and congresspeople spend a great deal of the taxpayers' money on travel to other countries. Do you think this is worthwhile? Why or why not?

_____

_____

_____

# GETTING ORGANIZED

Once you have read over the stimulus and understand what is being asked for, what is your next step in the essay test?

Because there is a strict time limit, many people want to start writing immediately. They are afraid that they won't finish the test if they don't spend the whole time writing. Generally, this is a poor strategy. People who start writing immediately without thinking or planning for a few minutes usually come up with very long, disorganized essays that do not accomplish their purpose. Remember—the quantity of your writing is <u>not</u> as important as the quality.

Since essay tests do have a time limit, you probably won't have time to write a detailed outline of what you plan to write. On the other hand, if you start writing right off the top of your head, your essay will be disorganized. Therefore, you need a way to plan quickly what you are going to write about.

**TEST HINT**

> After you have read the essay question carefully, take some time to jot down your ideas. This brainstorm list will help you get organized. This step also will help you focus on what you have to say about the given topic. Make this list your "plan" for what you are going to write. It doesn't have to be in any formal form—just write down ideas in a way that works best for you.

In this exercise, practice planning what you would say in each essay. <u>Do not write the essays.</u> Just get used to jotting down notes and ideas that you want to include in your paper. Think about each topic, then jot your ideas down in the space below it.

1. Smoking cigarettes has been determined to cause cancer. However, hundreds of thousands of people still smoke pack after pack of cigarettes. Why do you think people smoke although they know it is harmful? Support your explanation with specific details, reasons, and examples.

**CONTINUED**

**2.** Think of something you really like doing. In an essay, explain why you enjoy this activity and how you benefit from it. Give specific examples and reasons.

**3.** There are advantages and disadvantages to being married. There are also advantages and disadvantages to being single. Choose either "married life" or "single life" and write an essay that explains the advantages and disadvantages of this lifestyle. Be specific in your examples and ideas.

**4.** What do you think the most serious problem in the world is? Why? Write an essay explaining what you think and give specific examples and reasons.

# EXERCISE 3

# PUTTING IT ALL TOGETHER

Once you have taken a few minutes to write down your ideas on a topic, you should develop a plan for what you are going to say. Look over your list of ideas and see which ones are most important. Cross out any that don't really fit your plan. Add any ideas that occur to you. As you do these tasks, your plan for writing will become clearer to you.

**TEST HINT**

As you write your essay, refer back to your plan or brainstorm list from time to time. Also read over the essay stimulus you were given. Make sure you are staying on track in your writing. Are you answering the question? Are you including the important ideas you thought of?

In this exercise, choose one topic from Exercise 2 and write an essay on this topic. Write quickly, but be sure to include all important ideas.

# GIVING SPECIFIC EXAMPLES

As you have seen, in all essay assignments and tests it is important to be specific. When an essay stimulus asks you to give specific examples, what does this mean?

Giving examples is a good way to show your reader what you mean. For example, a statement like this is very general:

People litter because they are lazy.

In an essay, it could be improved by adding an example:

People litter because they are lazy. For example, it is easier to drop a lunch bag on the ground than it is to walk twenty yards to a trash barrel.

Specific examples help to show the reader exactly what you mean by a statement.

**TEST HINT**

When an essay question asks you to give specific examples, reasons, or details, be on the lookout for general statements in your writing. After these general ideas, add one or two specific examples of what you mean. This will really make your point clear to the reader.

In this exercise, imagine that you are writing an essay that asks you to provide specific examples. Under each general statement given, write one or two examples that clearly show the reader what is meant. The first one is done for you.

**1.** I prefer reading the newspaper over watching the news on TV.

*For example, I can read the newspaper whenever I want. I'd have to be home at 6 to watch the news on TV.*

_____

**2.** Many new jobs will be created if a sports arena is built in this town.

_____

_____

_____

*CONTINUED*

**3.** Capital punishment is fair only for people who commit very serious crimes.

_____

_____

_____

**4.** People love to watch soap operas about unhappy men and women.

_____

_____

_____

**5.** Having a lot of money is not always easy.

_____

_____

_____

**6.** There are different ways to help hungry and homeless people.

_____

_____

_____

**7.** My father always looks happy when we visit.

_____

_____

_____

**8.** The apartment was a mess.

_____

_____

_____

**9.** We should change the tax system in our country.

_____

_____

_____

# WRITING A REPORT FROM NOTES

Sometimes on an essay test or assignment, you may be asked to read over a bunch of notes and use them to write an essay. The notes are out of order, and some may not even belong in the essay. Your job is to organize these thoughts into a logical and understandable form for your reader.

This type of essay assignment is not too different from some of the brainstorming activities you have practiced in this book. What you really need to do is group ideas that belong together and get rid of irrelevant ideas. Refer to Exercises 12 and 14 in the warm-up section if you need to review these steps.

**TEST HINT**

Instead of starting to write right away, take a few minutes to group the ideas that should go in the same paragraph. Group them by circling or using numbers—whatever system you found most useful in brainstorming. Also, take a minute to cross out ideas that do not belong there.

Imagine that you have just attended a lecture given by a spokesperson from the city police department. She spoke about effective ways for pedestrians to prevent common theft. The neighborhood organization that you belong to has requested that you write up a report about the lecture. You took the following notes. Use these notes to write a short report.

- Officer Camille Rosen presented lecture
- three ways to avoid theft on the street
- pay attention to your surroundings
- know where you are heading
- carry only necessities
- put wallet in front pocket
- walk only in safe, well-lit places
- call loudly for help if you need it
- don't try to apprehend thief all by yourself
- carry only zippered purse and hold it close to you
- get a good look at the offender
- be aware of locations of police and fire departments

## EXERCISE 6

# USING PARAGRAPHS IN AN ESSAY TEST

When people write quickly, especially in a test situation, they sometimes forget to organize their writing. Many times, a final essay turns out to be one very long paragraph. The ideas in the essay might be good ones, but they are hard for the reader to understand because they are not organized well. When writing an essay test, you should avoid this problem.

How do you know when to start a new paragraph? How many paragraphs are "enough" for an essay test? Every essay is different, but here are some *general* guidelines that can help you organize your essays more effectively.

**TEST HINTS**

- <u>All</u> essays should have an introductory paragraph. This paragraph should let the reader know how you plan to answer the question.

- <u>Most</u> essays should have a concluding paragraph. In this paragraph, you sum up the main points you have made in the essay and perhaps leave the reader with something extra to think about.

- Try to write one paragraph for each major idea you have to discuss. If, for example, you have three reasons for a point of view, put each reason into its own paragraph. If you are explaining a process, try dividing the steps into two or three main sections, each section in its own paragraph.

  There is no firm rule for paragraphing, but try to divide your writing into organized pieces that your reader will follow easily. In general, a paragraph should contain four to six sentences.

In this exercise, read each topic and take some time to think about how you would organize each essay. Decide how many paragraphs you would write on this topic. Then, briefly outline what information would be included in each paragraph. <u>Do not write the essay.</u> Hold on to your work because you will need it again in a later exercise. The first item is done for you.

**1.** Should television advertising be banned during children's shows and cartoons? Write an essay telling what you think and why.

*Paragraph 1:*      *introduction that states my opinion: no, TV ads should not be banned*

*Paragraph 2:*    *my first reason for this opinion: manufacturers have an equal right to airtime*

*Paragraph 3:*    *another reason: advertising informs the public*

*Paragraph 4:*    *a conclusion: banning this advertising would be unfair to all*

**2.** If you were going on an endless trip to another planet, what two modern conveniences would you take with you? Why?

**3.** Many people think that taxes are unfair to the working citizen. These people believe that their tax money should not go toward welfare for the poor or care for the elderly. They do not think that they should be forced to help such people.

   Do you agree or disagree that all citizens have an obligation to assist those citizens in need? Give reasons to support your point of view.

**4.** Think of a person with whom you are very close. Describe this person's *physical* features to someone who does not know this person. Try to be so specific that your reader would be able to pick this person out of a crowd just by reading your description.

**5.** People undergo many changes in the course of their lives. Some changes, like getting older, are expected. Others, like a sudden death or a bitter divorce, are completely unexpected. It seems that some people are more able to cope with change than other people. They can more easily "bounce back" and adjust to their new situation.

   Explain why some people find change easier than others. What can people do to become more comfortable with the changes in their lives? Support your explanation with details and examples.

# EXERCISE 7

# YOU BE THE READER

 As you write for a test or even an in-class writing assignment, remember that someone will be reading and grading your paper. You must make your ideas clear and organized so that the reader will have no difficulty understanding what you mean.

What does a reader look for when he reads a test essay? He looks for many things that are characteristic of good writing. The hints below will help you keep in mind what is important in reading (and writing!) an essay.

**TEST HINTS**

Essay test readers look for answers to these kinds of questions.

- Did the writer answer the question?
- Did he make his position clear?
- Did he give <u>specific</u> reasons, examples, and details to support his points?
- Is the writing organized so that it can be followed and understood easily?
- Is the writing free from errors in grammar, punctuation, and spelling?

In this exercise, you are the reader and grader of the essays below. Use the hints above to help you decide how effective each essay is. On a separate sheet of paper, write down the answers to the questions above. Based on these answers, decide whether you think the writer has done a good job on the essay. Write *good, satisfactory*, or *needs improvement* next to each essay.

> **ESSAY QUESTION:** Name two people who have had an influence on you, either good or bad. Tell what their influence was and how it affected you.

**1.** One person who really influenced me during my childhood was my mother. Unfortunately, she was not a good influence at all. Ever since I can remember, she was coming and going from our home whenever it suited her. She left my brothers and me alone with my father for days at a time. It seems that she never really wanted children and was never really planning to settle down at all. She had several different boyfriends, and she traveled all over with them. My father would beg her to stay home with him, and sometimes she would, for a week or even a month. Then she'd get restless again and head off on another fling.

**2.** The two people who have had the most influence on me are Helen Keller and my grandfather. Helen Keller was a woman who overcame severe physical disabilities, while my grandfather is a man who used all his energy and resources to help other people.

Helen Keller could have easily given up on life. She was born unable to see, hear, or speak. At first, she led a very sheltered life, but gradually she emerged from it with the help of a skilled and dedicated teacher. She learned to communicate through her sense of touch and through sign language. This courageous woman then went on to teach others with similar disabilities.

My grandfather is a truly great man as well. In all my life, I have never met a more generous and loving person. He has really affected me in many ways.

**3.** There are many people who have had an influence on my life, but two stand out more than others. One is a younger sister, and the other is an older sister. It is difficult to say whether their influences were good or bad, but it is clear that they both made me a stronger person.

As we were growing up, my younger sister was always in trouble. I always had to be on my toes, ready and able to get her out of one mess or another. This experience has made me better able to help my sons and daughters when they need it.

My older sister was the role model for our family. I was always striving to be more like her. Her influence made me more competitive—wanting to be better all the time.

**4.** Two people who have had an influence in my life are my ex-wife and Bruce Springsteen. My ex-wife has done nothing but make my life miserable. She has made me insecure and restless with my life. Springsteen, on the other hand, is a man who speaks to me from the heart. His words and music give me strength and hope that my life will someday turn around.

Before I met my ex-wife, I was content with myself. I had good friends, and I liked my job. Even though I was only a construction worker, I felt like I had something to offer. But then she came along and took it all away. She made me feel stupid and worthless—so much that I started wondering if I had anything going for me. My friends stayed away because she made them feel lousy too. When she left me, I knew it was the best thing, but I still don't have my old confidence back.

On a more positive side, I like to write poetry, and I have learned a lot from the work of Bruce Springsteen. In many a bad time, I can turn on his music and feel better about myself and the rest of the world. He speaks to people like me who don't always have an easy time of things. Somehow, he lets you know that there is always good with the bad and that things will get better.

# REVISING YOUR ESSAY IN A TEST SITUATION

Hopefully, if you have planned well, you will have a few minutes left after you complete your essay. This time should be spent revising and editing your work.

*Revising* means going back over your writing to make sure you have accomplished what you wanted to. (*Editing*, which you will learn more about in the next activity, is more like fine-tuning, in which you correct spelling and grammar errors.) At the revision stage, you take out ideas that don't belong there, add ideas that would help make your point, and possibly change the order of things.

Because you don't have unlimited time to revise, you should resist the temptation to cross out and rewrite huge sections of what you have written. The initial planning and organization you did in the beginning of the test period will probably make this unnecessary. Instead, use these hints for revising in a test situation:

**TEST HINTS**

- Make sure your writing is organized into clear and concise paragraphs, including a strong introductory one. If you see a long paragraph that has too many different ideas in it, break it up into two or three shorter ones. Do this by writing this symbol (¶) where you would like a new paragraph.

- Look for ideas that should be taken out or moved somewhere else. Sometimes a sentence would make more sense if it appeared in a different paragraph. Neatly circle this sentence and draw an arrow where you think it should go. Other times, a sentence may turn out to be irrelevant to the topic: Cross it out, but do it neatly so that the reader will have no trouble understanding the words around it.

- Try not to make more than one or two changes in the revision stage. Don't forget that your paper should be easy to read and understand.

In this exercise, go back to an essay you planned in Exercise 6. Take about fifteen minutes to write the essay. Then, use the hints above to help you revise your writing. Since you won't have a great deal of time, limit your revisions to two or three changes that would really affect your overall paper. Try to complete your revisions in five minutes.

# EDITING YOUR ESSAY IN A TEST SITUATION

Your essay will be easier to read and understand if it is free of errors in grammar, punctuation, and spelling. Terrific ideas in a paper mean nothing if the reader can't understand them. This is why it is important to use correct English at all times.

Editing your writing is the last step in taking an essay test. If you try to go back and fix words and sentences as you write, you will probably be unable to get all your thoughts down in the time allotted. You may end up with five perfectly written sentences, but this means nothing if you have not gotten your whole point across. <u>Finish saying what you want to say *before* you go back to edit.</u>

Of course, editing will be easier if you wrote carefully the first time around. As you write, try to use correct grammar and think about the spelling of words as you use them. However, you shouldn't spend a great deal of time deciding whether to use a comma or debating over how to spell a difficult word. These issues can be taken care of if you have time after you complete your essay. These hints should help you in editing an essay test:

**TEST HINTS**

- Don't start editing until you are satisfied with your essay as a whole. Once you consider your piece complete, then go over each sentence looking for errors.

- If you know you have several mistakes in your writing, but don't have the time to fix them all, try to fix the ones that stand out the most. <u>Do this neatly.</u>

- Incomplete and run-on sentences are often the hardest to read and understand, so make these corrections a priority.

- Spelling is important, but if you truly do not know how to spell a word, do your best and move on to more editing. One or two incorrectly spelled words will not ruin your essay. Essay scorers are aware that you do not have the luxury of time and a dictionary.

In this exercise, go back and edit the essay you wrote in Exercise 8. Use the hints above to help you and don't spend more than three or four minutes on editing.

# EXERCISE 10

# THE PRACTICE ESSAY

The following items represent samples of different kinds of essay questions you may encounter on tests. Use them to practice your test taking skills.

You have one half hour to write on each topic. Do only one essay in a sitting—if you do more, you will become tired and your writing will not be your best.

Remember to use the same plan you have learned in this section:

- Organize your ideas.
- Write the essay.
- Read over your paper and make changes.
- Edit your work, being sure to correct as many grammar and spelling errors as possible.

As in a real test situation, do not use any books when you write your essay.

1. A group of developers is considering building a shopping mall in a large field in your community. Some of your neighbors want the mall to be built because they feel it will bring new jobs and greater prosperity to the area. Others, however, are angry with the building proposal. They prefer the land to be left as it is. These people dread the noise, traffic, and confusion the mall would bring.

   Write an essay that either supports or opposes the building of the mall. Take only one point of view and defend it with specific examples and reasons.

2. Living in the city has many advantages and disadvantages. Living in a suburb or out in the country has different advantages and disadvantages. Write an essay on the advantages and disadvantages of either living in a city or living out of a city. Make sure you give specific examples and reasons.

3. There are people in the world who regularly do things that endanger their lives. For example, one man attempts to go over Niagara Falls in a barrel for the second time. Very few people have survived such a stunt. Another man drives a motorcycle across a large canyon, and another performs dangerous skydiving tricks.

   Explain why people would put their own lives in danger. What makes them want to live in this way? Support your explanation with specific details and examples.

**4.** Many people in the United States are strongly in favor of a policy of "equal pay for comparable work." This policy means that everyone should get the same pay for work that involves the same level of skills, knowledge, and responsibility. For example, a school secretary, with a high school diploma and four years experience, should be paid the same as the school groundskeeper, who also has a high school diploma and four years experience.

Other people, however, think that this is not a good policy. They think it is too difficult to compare different jobs and that some jobs are just more difficult than others.

The average salary for a second-year nurse is less than the average salary for a second-year prison guard. Do you think this is fair? Write an essay that gives your opinion of the "equal pay for comparable work" policy. Be sure to defend your position with clear reasons and examples. reasons and examples.

**5.** Think of some important event in your life. It could be something that happened to you or something that happened to someone else that affected you in some way. Write an essay that tells what happened and why it was important to you.

**6.** A person tells a "white lie" when he says something that is untrue but harmless. For example, when you eat at a friend's house, you might say that everything was delicious, when in fact, you really disliked the food. This kind of lie doesn't seem to hurt anyone, and it may even have spared the cook's feelings.

Are "white lies" acceptable? Or should people tell the truth in all circumstances? Explain what are acceptable types of white lies, if there are any. Give reasons and examples to support your explanation.

**7.** Some people prefer to keep their feelings and emotions inside. They rely on their own strengths and abilities to overcome most obstacles. Others seek guidance and relief by letting their feelings out in the open. These people find that holding everything inside is not the answer when they have problems.

Write an essay telling whether it is better to keep troublesome emotions inside or to share them with others. Give specific examples, details, and reasons.

**8.** Think of an event that changed your mind about something. Before this event, you thought one thing; after the event, you thought something different. Write an essay about this event and how it changed your thinking.

# ANSWERS

## WARM-UP AND PREWRITING

### EXERCISE 4

A. 4
B. 2
C. 1
D. 5
E. 3

### EXERCISE 8

You should have crossed out these ideas:
1. diet
   gym shoes
2. saw accident last week
   if you don't drive, there's no way to get home
3. basic training is a drag
   the uniform is ugly

### EXERCISE 11

1. B, I, C
2. C, I, B
3. C, B, I
4. I, C, B

### EXERCISE 12

1. *UNIFYING IDEA:* transportation

   *HEADING 1:* air
   helicopter, Goodyear blimp, airplane

   *HEADING 2:* land
   jeep, bicycle, station wagon

   *HEADING 3:* water
   yacht, canoe, sailboat

2. *UNIFYING IDEA:* food

   *HEADING 1:* meat
   steak, hamburgers, meatloaf

   *HEADING 2:* vegetables
   string beans, corn, potatoes

   *HEADING 3:* drinks
   beer, red wine, soda pop

3. *UNIFYING IDEA:* job experience

   *HEADING 1:* outdoor jobs
   mowed lawns, delivered newspapers, shoveled snow

**HEADING 2:** industrial jobs
operated forklift, was a
metal worker, ran
factory assembly
line

**HEADING 3:** bank jobs
was a bank teller, was a
loan officer,
promoted to
bank vp

**4. UNIFYING IDEA:** reasons to vote for this
candidate

**HEADING 1:** experience
has held other offices, worked
in government for 15 years,
had experience as mayor's
assistant

**HEADING 2:** good economic policies
promises to lower taxes, has
good ideas to promote
business, will get budget
under control

**HEADING 3:** personal characteristics
cares about our town, will work
hard for us, is honest and
trustorworthy

## EXERCISE 13

**UNIFYING STATEMENT:** It's unfair that trash is collected so infrequently in this community.

I. Garbage hurts the neighborhood's appearance.
   A. it's depressing to look at
   B. streets look like a tornado hit them
   C. we want to be proud of street's appearance
   D. it makes us look like slobs

II. Excess trash is a health hazard.
   A. bad for the environment
   B. apartments here have more roaches due to trash
   C. kids get sick from playing near trash

III. Other neighborhoods get better trash collection service.
   A. no garbage in front of mayor's house
   B. garbage pickup is better in Salem Heights
   C. wealthy suburbs are spotless

# NARRATIVE WRITING

## EXERCISE 2

**1.** 4, 2, 5, 3, 1
**2.** 3, 2, 4, 5, 1
**3.** 2, 1, 3, 5, 4
**4.** 3, 1, 4, 5, 2